AF674617

Catch And Play With The Words

Use proper words,

Change Your Life

Written and Illustrated by

Danish Tyagi

CONTENT

Chapter:01

Introduction

Word can be introduced as symbol for

communication with one another. It is essential for verbal communication, present our thoughts, share our feelings and passing or conveying information. More than one word makes a sentence and a word consists of different characters, some characters it self works as an word like "." means pause or break. or silence. In this chapter I will provide you dear reader a introduction of word which play a important role in everyone's daily routine life, in general most of us are not properly using words while communicating, presenting our thoughts, sharing our feelings and passing or conveying information with or to anyone. I have observed many persons are not selecting proper word, taking too much pauses, use similar word (whose speech essence are seems same).

Many questions are coming in the mind when I am observing while people are communicating to each other like

- What he/she want to say?
- What he/she understanding?
- What he/she want to write?
- What he/she want to indicate?
- Is he/she aware with other's current situation?
- Is his/her words are suitable in current situation?
- What was conclusion of whole communication?

Similarly, multiple type of questions is raised by mind and inspired me to write something on 'word'. By reading this book you people will get a support for using word in communication. Every time it is not necessary to say or write something, sometime silence or full stop says everything.

In verbal communication, mostly people are not focusing where they have to take pause, which word required more pressure and how much voice volume to be maintain while talking to any one. Regular floating words in environment is not make sense that communication is effective and material which was required to deliver that has been delivered successfully instead of floating words continuously we should think what we want to say and deliver to other, for we should think for a moment and select suitable with reference to content, after selecting proper words further we should say and float our words and complete our communication in minimum time.

In written communication, mostly people are not facing challenge what they have to write?, how to start writing something?, is my grammar is proper or not?, instead of wasting our time in too much thinking we should start writing and read the content what we had write and check is it delivering our thought or not?, If content have sense as per our thought just pass written message to other person, if content not making any sense take help our other person but content writing is required, since it builds a basic building block of written communication corrections may be happen in future.

Chapter:02

Why Words are important?

Words importance can be addressed as two persons are sitting on a single bench like John and Tim but both were silent for more than 30min, in this time period no written message, no sign language used, and no word said by both. This not a any kind of communication it is just like two non-living things kept on bench. Thus, word are important for communication. Words are used to pass information, express our thoughts, and write something. Dear reader you are thinking what is the use of words for deaf and dump, blind persons?, answer for this query is just this they are using sign language and every sign is related to a word, so as per expressed sign by them other person can translate the meaning what they want. If a question also comes in mind related to animals, birds and new born baby what is the use of words for these?, as per our or same species requirement we or same species trained animal, birds and new born babies they express there feeling by expressions or acting on words. Thus, words play a important role in routine line.

Chapter:03

Positive Words

Words positivity can be observed when a person receives those words from other person and his facial expression get change with full of glimpses. The positive words provides strength to people to do something more, most of leaders uses positive words towards there team and family members which supports the listeners, teammates provides there supports is future projects as well and family members provides there support while a person is in troubles.

Positive words are important to express for compiling activity for others as well, someone appreciating and using positive words these makes people mind in positive direction that his/her efforts are acknowledged by someone. This positive-ness increases the priority level towards us means appreciator.

It is required whenever we are communicating to any other person we should use positive words, although we know that the person nature is not good.

The positive words changes persons mind set if he/she was not supporting you, after using positive you people will observe others will support you and listen you. We can use below positive words:

---

able accepting adaptable bold

brave calm caring cheerful

clever complex confident dependable

dignified	empathetic	energetic	extroverted
friendly	giving	happy	helpful
idealistic	independent	ingenious	intelligent
introverted	kind	knowledgeable	logical
loving	mature	modest	nervous
observant	organized	patient	powerful
proud	quiet	reflective	relaxed
religious	responsive	searching	self-assertive
self-conscious	sensible	sentimental	shy
silly	spontaneous	sympathetic	tense
trustworthy	warm	wise	witty

Chapter:04

Negative Words

Words negativity can be observed when a person receives those words from other person and his facial expression get change with full of tension or sorrow. The negative words losses the strength of people to do something more, and raises a question what should I do next?, fills person in troubles.

Negative words are important to express for provide correction in very important thing or activity which have savior impact on others. These are used for making people disciplined, follow a track or rules and make environment healthy.

It is required whenever we are communicating to any other person we should not use negative words until it's requirement.

We know the person nature is good but if that person is not responding you after several time approaching and task is very much important than we can negative words to change his/her mental state and accelerate mind.

Without reason smile

Idle Person

Always unhappy

Do something

The negative words changes persons mind set if he/she was not supporting you, after using negative words you people will observe others will support you and listen you. We can use below negative words:

- Filthy
- No
- Noxious
- Disheveled
- Harmful
- Disappointed
- Embarrassed
- Jealous
- No one
- Decaying
- Beneath
- Missing
- Deny
- Immature
- Perturb
- Yucky
- Bad
- Lousy
- Reptilian
- Disgusting

- Old
- Inane
- Repugnant
- Lose
- Malicious
- Naive
- Jealous
- Abysmal
- Nasty
- Mean
- Stinky
- Fight
- Cutting
- Zero
- Petty
- Unfair
- Shoddy
- Vindictive
- Boring
- Apathy

Pessimism Fear Sad

Destroy No Expensive

Bleak Stop Weakness

Bad Confused

Hate Negative Lose

Deceit Down Anger

Despair Worse Poor

Poverty Cannot Fake

Wrong Backwards Stupid

Disaster Lazy

Jaded

Fall

Chapter:05

Words Selection

Words selection refers to the specific selection of words a writer or speaker uses to convey meaning, tone, and clarity in communication. It significantly impacts readability and engagement, making it crucial for effective writing, whether in essays, articles, or any other form of written communication. By carefully choosing words, one can ensure precision and evoke the desired response or emotion from the audience.

In my opinion a speaker, in general, is most careful about the word selection. An improper word choice leads to a certain misunderstanding. The worst situation would be that the audience and words receiver start to revolt.

In this chapter, we are going to study word selection.

Whenever be we are communicating with any other person we should remember a beautiful word need to be selected in communication and make communication conclusive. Words should be simple and understandable, reduce the use of short forms and make sentences complete. Selecting words involves understanding and correctly applying the rules of context to choose the most suitable words. It tests an individual's grasp of vocabulary and context, and their ability to effectively communicate meaningfully. This skill is vital for enhancing the quality of written and spoken language. Selecting the correct word from a set of options often requires critical thinking, social communication, political speech, build strong relationships and problem-solving skills. One analyzes the given criteria, considers the context, and makes informed decisions, developing their analytical thinking, reasoning, and decision-making abilities. Selecting words requires you to choose the optimal word or phrase out of list to fill in the sentence or statement.

All the people you are communicating with do not have the same level of vocabulary, knowledge, or values. They don't have the same level of knowledge, hence by following chapter 03 and chapter 04 one can easily select positive or negative word as per your requirement.

In daily use of words is essential in developing fluency and effective communication skills. By incorporating new words into your daily life conversations, you can expand your vocabulary and improve your ability to express yourself clearly. Whether you are speaking with friends, colleagues, or clients, having a wide range of vocabulary at your disposal allows you to convey your thoughts and ideas more precisely.

Chapter:06

Words And Practical Situation

Words utilization and practical situation are interlink with each other as when we are making any communication we should analyses the situation of environment means romantic environment, funny environment, happy environment and sad environment etc. according to environment condition we should utilize the words. Sometime we have to change environment by using words like sad environment created by somebody due any issue, so it can be changed in funny environment by using positive and funny words.

The specific selection of words a writer or speaker

uses impacts on environment. By carefully choosing words, one can ensure precision and evoke the desired response or emotion from the audience. The speaker's or writer's words can make a environment healthy or worst or vice-versa means as per environment condition speaker's or writer's health can be change like in sorrow environment if a writer or speaker uses words for jokes which can be objectionable by others. Thus, words selection is necessary while communicating in practical world as it is depending on words have a profound and multifaceted impact in practical situations, shaping our interactions, influencing decisions, and affecting outcomes in countless ways. Here's are key impacts which supports in handling practical situation:

1. Conveying Information Situation: The most basic impact is the transmission of facts, ideas, instructions, and opinions. Clear and precise language

ensures accurate understanding and reduces the risk of misinterpretations in the environment.

2. Building Shared Meaning: Words allow us to create common ground and shared understanding with others. This is crucial for collaboration, teamwork, and building relationships.

3. Expressing Emotional Situation: Words enable us to articulate our feelings, whether joy, sadness, anger, or fear. This allows for emotional connection and empathy.

4. Asking Questions and Seeking Clarification: Words are essential for gathering information, resolving doubts, and ensuring everyone is on the same page in the group or environment.

5. Motivational Situations: Carefully chosen words can inspire, encourage, and motivate individuals or groups to take specific actions. You need to think of powerful speeches or compelling marketing campaigns.

6. Building Trust and Credibility: Consistent and honest communication fosters trust and establishes credibility. This is essential for long-term relationships and effective leadership.

7. Framing Perceptions: The way we frame information using specific words can significantly impact how others perceive a situation or person. This can be used both constructively and manipulatively.

8. Building Connections: Kind, supportive, and empathetic words can strengthen bonds and create positive relationships.

9. Resolving Conflicts: Skillful communication, using words to understand perspectives and find common ground, is crucial for conflict resolution.

10. Damaging Relationships: Harsh, critical, or insensitive words can cause hurt, resentment, and damage trust, potentially leading to the breakdown of relationships.

11. Establishing Social Norms and Expectations: Language plays a role in defining acceptable behavior and setting expectations within social groups and organizations.

12. Analyzing Situations: Words allow us to describe, analyze, and categorize information, which is essential for understanding complex situations.

13. Documenting Agreements and Plans: Written words provide a record of decisions, agreements, and plans, ensuring clarity and accountability.

14. Business situations: A well-crafted sales pitch can secure a deal. A poorly worded email can lead to misunderstandings with a client. Constructive feedback can improve employee performance.

15. Healthcare situations: Clear communication between doctors and patients is crucial for accurate diagnosis and effective treatment. Empathetic language can provide comfort and support.

16. Educational Situations: Teachers use language to impart knowledge, guide discussions, and assess student understanding. The way feedback is given can significantly impact a student's motivation.

17. Personal Relationships: Expressing love and appreciation strengthens bonds. Apologizing sincerely can repair hurt feelings. Constructive criticism, delivered with care, can help loved ones grow.

Words are have tangible impacts on our lives and the world around us. Being mindful of the words we choose and how we use them is essential for effective communication, building strong relationships, achieving our goals, and navigating the complexities of practical situations.

Chapter:07

Power of Words

Words are so strong that can fill happiness or deep sadness in someone's life. Words have a profound and multifaceted impact in practical situations, shaping our interactions, influencing decisions, and affecting outcomes in countless ways.

Power of words:

1. Improve Communication and Understanding: The transmission of facts, ideas, instructions, and opinions have major impact. Words allow us to create common ground and shared understanding with others. This is crucial for collaboration, teamwork, and building relationships. Words enable us to articulate our

feelings, whether joy, sadness, anger, or fear. This allows for emotional connection and empathy. Words are essential for gathering information, resolving doubts, and ensuring everyone is on the same page.

2. Influence and Persuasion to others: Words can inspire, encourage, and motivate individuals or groups to take specific actions. This is vital in areas like sales, negotiation, and social change. Consistent and honest communication fosters trust and establishes credibility. This is essential for long-term relationships and effective leadership.

3. Build Strong Relationships and Social Dynamics: Kind, supportive, and empathetic words can strengthen bonds and create positive relationships. The way we frame information using specific words can significantly impact how others perceive a situation or person. This can be used both constructively and manipulatively.

4. Improve Decision-Making and Problem-Solving: Words allow us to describe, analyze, and categorize information, which is essential for understanding complex situations. Brainstorming and discussing ideas using language are fundamental to the problem-solving process. Words help us articulate the pros and cons of different choices and make informed decisions. Written words provide a record of decisions, agreements, and plans, ensuring clarity and accountability.

5. Develop Personal and Self-Perception: The words we use internally influences our self-perception, beliefs about our capabilities, and overall mindset. Positive self-talk can be empowering, while negative self-talk can be limiting.

Articulating our goals and intentions using words helps to clarify our focus and increase the likelihood of achieving them. Language is the primary tool for learning new information and expanding our understanding of the world.

6. Handle Practical Situations:

A. Business: A well-crafted sales pitch can secure a deal. A poorly worded email can lead to misunderstandings with a client. Constructive feedback can improve employee performance.

B. Healthcare: Clear communication between doctors and patients is crucial for accurate diagnosis and effective treatment. Empathetic language can provide comfort and support.

C. Education: Teachers use language to impart knowledge, guide discussions, and assess student understanding. The way feedback is given can significantly impact a student's motivation.

D. Personal Relationships: Expressing love and appreciation strengthens bonds. Apologizing sincerely can repair hurt feelings. Constructive criticism, delivered with care, can help loved ones grow.

E. Negotiations: Skillful use of language, including active listening and persuasive arguments, can lead to favorable outcomes.

Chapter:08

Importance of Silence

Words are not always require for communication

sometime silence require. Silent communication happens when you don't use words or sounds during a conversation. According to Carolyn Ellis, "When used with intention and purpose, silence is a communication superpower."

Silence can also be positive or negative. For instance, positive silence can be constructive by helping to move a conversation forward, change the subject, or indicate an endpoint to the verbal exchange. In contrast, negative silence can be destructive by shutting down communication or relaying hostility. It can also be used as the "silent treatment" by people who shut down when emotions run high.

Benefits and importance

Communicating silently has many advantages. These are as follows:

1. Promotes healthy communication in relationships: As long as it's positive silence, staying quiet can help you listen to your partner, make them feel heard, and express your comfort within the relationship. Also, remaining silent can help prevent disagreements from escalating.

2. Fosters active listening: Effective communication often breaks down when the listener is busy formulating their response in their head instead of really listening to what the other person has to say. Pausing and focusing on the deeper meaning of what the person is trying to convey can help you comprehend and understand before responding.

3. Supports effective negotiations: When used at certain points in a negotiation, silence can relay confidence and strength. It can also leave space for others to speak. However, it can create an uncomfortable feeling that may pressure others to fill the void with talking. Knowing when to ask questions and when to leave space for others to speak can help you more effectively assess the needs of others in a negotiation.

Disadvantages

Despite its benefits, silent communication can have negative effects too. These are as follows:

1. Silence can cause miscommunication: Silence during a conversation can convey several meanings, which can differ among individuals. It can also express anger or hostility unintentionally. Remaining quiet when someone asks you a question can confuse the questioner about how you feel.

2. Negative silent communication can be toxic:

Strategies like the silent treatment, when one person shuts off communication with another out of anger, can be destructive to self-esteem and harm relationships. People with narcissistic personality disorder may use this tactic to control and manipulate others.

Silence is a highly productive communication tool on its own. The trick is to use it appropriately. Here's how:

- Use gestures: When silently listening to others, use your eyes, gestures, and posture to convey interest. For example, continue eye contact if that is something the other person is comfortable with, and nod to indicate you acknowledge what they are saying.

- Pause before speaking: During an important conversation, like a job interview, allow a few seconds to pass before you answer questions. This can prevent you from divulging too much unnecessary information and give you time to formulate an appropriate response.

- Use silence for effect: You can use silence to add weight to your statements. For instance, try pausing for a moment after you've said something powerful and important to you to allow your message to sink in.
- Practice active listening with silence: For example, while you remain quiet in a conversation, consider making a conscious effort to understand the underlying thoughts, feelings, and ideas the other person is trying to communicate.

Dear reader silent communication used in this way will most likely lead to communication breakdown and, in some cases, could be considered abusive. Silence comes naturally. These fortunate individuals know the power of silence and they are comfortable in that silence.

There are quite a few of us who need to learn the art

of practicing silence. Read on for more reasons to try silence in your daily communications.

1. Silence gets people's attention: When the speaker stops talking a signal goes to the brain that something has happened. All of the sudden you pay attention to try and figure out why communication has stopped. The same is true in our daily conversations. If we are silent, people take note and we gain their attention.

2. Silence can be an obvious answer: Sometimes when we communicate we say too much. We over-explain. If a question is met with silence, there is often an answer in that silence. We can also soften the blow of a negative answer by silence being the response. There is an implied "no" without any harsh words or too many words that might do more harm than good.

3. Silence uses nonverbal language: Often our nonverbal language is a more powerful way of communicating than our verbal language. According

to HelpGuide.org, "It's important to recognize, though, that it's our nonverbal communication - our facial expressions, gestures, eye contact, posture, and ton of voice - that speaks the loudest. The ability to understand and use nonverbal communication , or body language, is a powerful tool that can help you connect with others, express what you really mean, and build better relationships."

4. Silence offers empathy to others: There are times in life where silence offers empathy and understanding to others. Sometimes we don't have the right words to communicate to someone who is struggling with a hurtful or sorrowful situation. We can show someone we care and we are there for them without using a plethora of words. We can offer comfort by our calming silence.

5. Silence is polite: We are silent we give others a chance to speak. We show them that they matter.

At last we can be effective communicators by utilizing our ability to be silent. There is great strength in silence. Now, we just need to keep practicing. Like the old adages go practice makes perfect and silence is golden.

Chapter:09

Use Words Precisely

Words use matters what we want to pass message to anyone are not always require for communication for our audience, message, and purpose; of writing constructively; and of writing persuasively. Every word should have a distinct and useful purpose. For writing constructively 7 C's can be applied for good results in writing that is Clear, Coherent, Concise, Concrete, Correct, Complete and Courteous.

CLEAR writing involves knowing what you want to say before you say it because often a lack of clarity comes from unclear thinking or poor planning, clear writing conveys the purpose of the document immediately to the reader; it matches vocabulary to the audience, avoiding jargon and unnecessary technical or obscure language while at the same time being precise. In clarifying your ideas, ensure that each sentence conveys one idea, and that each paragraph thoroughly develops one unified concept.

COHERENT writing ensures that the reader can easily follow your ideas and your train of thought. One idea should lead logically into the next through the use of transitional words and phrases, structural markers, planned repetition, sentences with clear subjects, headings that are clear, and effective and parallel lists. Writing that lacks coherence often sounds "choppy" and ideas seem disconnected or incomplete. Coherently connecting ideas is like building bridges between islands of thought so the reader can easily move from one idea to the next.

CONCISE writing uses the least words possible to convey the most meaning while still maintaining clarity.

Avoid unnecessary padding, awkward phrasing, overuse of "to be" forms (is, are, was, were, am, be, being), long preposition strings, vagueness, unnecessary repetition and redundancy. Use active verbs whenever possible, and take the time to choose a single word rather than a long phrase expression. Think of your word count like a budget; be cost effective by making sure every word you choose does effective work for you.

CONCRETE writing involves using specific, precise language to paint a picture for your readers so that they can more easily understand your ideas. If you have to explain an abstract concept or idea, try to use examples, analogies, and precise language to illustrate it. Use measurable descriptors whenever possible; avoid vague terms like "big" or "good." Try to get your readers to "see" your ideas by using specific terms and descriptions.

CORRECT writing uses standard language punctuation, sentence structure, usage, and grammar. Being correct also means providing accurate information, as well as using the right document type and form for the task.

COMPLETE writing includes all requested information and answers all relevant questions. The more concrete and specific you are, the more likely your document will be complete as well. Review your checklist of specifications before submitting your document to its intended reader.

COURTEOUS writing entails designing a reader-friendly, easy-to-read document; using tactful language and appropriate modes of addressing the audience; and avoiding potentially offensive terminology, usage, and tone.

The more word choices you have in your vocabulary, the more likely you will communicate with clarity. The words you choose to use will have subtlety and depth, conveying more precisely and efficiently what it is you want to say.

Listen: Consciously collecting words from conversations around you is another excellent method of picking up vocabulary. If you hear an unfamiliar word and can't deduce its meaning through context clues ask for an explanation. Most people are only too happy to give one. If possible have them write it down so you can check it thoroughly later.

Changing one word in a sentence can dramatically increase its impact.

Most writers keep using the same words. This produces boring content. Doesn't engage the reader. And causes low read rates.

At the end while writing and speaking we should select words with have suitable timing and tone during use and not to be repeat again and again, these shall be used precisely and make sentences conclusive, not to be open ended communication.

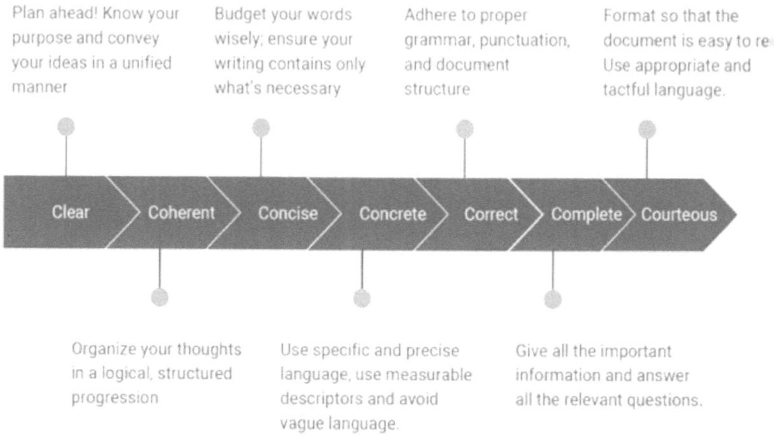

Chapter:10

Make words in strength

Words in a sentence can dramatically increase its impact. In the world of effective communication, the power of words cannot be underestimated. Whether it's conveying ideas, influencing others, or inspiring action, the key to impactful communication lies in the ability to make words more powerful. By understanding the techniques and strategies that empower our words, individuals can unlock a newfound level of influence and make their communication resonate with others on a deeper level.

When your words are clear and concise, you ensure that your message is easily understood by your audience. Clarity eliminates misunderstandings, reduces confusion, and enhances overall comprehension. Clear communication requires careful thought and consideration of your audience.

Think about the purpose of your message and tailor it to suit the needs and knowledge level of your listeners or readers. Avoid using jargon or technical terms that may not be familiar to your audience. Instead, opt for simple and straightforward language that can be easily grasped.

Additionally, organizing your thoughts in a logical and coherent manner contributes to clarity. Consider the structure of your message, whether it's a speech, email, or article, and break it down into clear sections or points. This helps your audience follow along easily, ensuring that your message is not lost in a sea of information.

You should ensure that your words have the maximum

impact and effectively convey your intended message.

A strong vocabulary is key to honing your communication skills and making your words more powerful. A wide range of words opens up a multitude of possibilities for expressing yourself effectively and leaving a lasting impact on your listeners or readers. Dear readers when you expand your vocabulary, you gain access to a variety of words that carry different nuances and shades of meaning. This allows you to articulate your thoughts more precisely, making your message more impactful and engaging. Moreover, using a diverse vocabulary shows that you are well-educated and can command the attention of your audience. One way to enhance your word choice is by reading extensively. Explore various genres, both fiction and non-fiction, to expose yourself to different styles of writing and a wide array of vocabulary. Make a habit of noting down unfamiliar words and their meanings, and then actively incorporate them into your daily vocabulary.

Another helpful way is to practice using synonyms and antonyms. This not only improves your vocabulary but also helps you understand the subtle differences in meaning between words. Additionally, using metaphors and similes can add depth and richness to your communication. Building a strong vocabulary is essential for making your words more powerful.

Crafting compelling messages is a crucial skill in impactful communication. It involves structuring your words in a way that captures attention and resonates with your audience. By understanding the key elements of effective communication, you can create messages that leave a lasting impact.

To craft compelling messages, start by defining your objective. What do you want to achieve with your communication? Whether it's to inform, persuade, or inspire, having a clear objective will help you structure your message accordingly.

Next, consider your audience. Tailor your message to their needs, interests, and level of understanding. This will make your words more relatable and engaging. Use language that is appropriate and accessible to your audience, avoiding jargon or complex terms that might alienate them.

Structuring your message with a strong introduction is vital. Capture attention with a compelling hook or a thought-provoking question. Then, present your main points in a logical and organized manner, using headings or bullet points to enhance readability.

Support your message with evidence, facts, or personal anecdotes to make it more persuasive and credible. Use storytelling techniques to evoke emotions and connect on a deeper level with your audience. End with a clear call to action, guiding your audience on what to do next.

Crafting compelling messages is a skill that can be honed through practice and feedback. By mastering the art of structuring your communication effectively, you can make your words more powerful and impactful.

While words convey meaning, our body language and gestures can enhance or detract from the message we intend to deliver. Understanding and utilizing body language effectively can significantly increase the power of our words.

Body language includes facial expressions, hand

movements, posture, eye contact, and tone of voice. When used consciously, these nonverbal cues can help convey confidence, sincerity, and authority. For example, maintaining eye contact during a conversation signifies attentiveness and engagement, while slouching or fidgeting can undermine your credibility.

Being aware of your own body language is crucial, but it is equally important to interpret and respond to the nonverbal cues of others. If someone crosses their arms or avoids eye contact, they may be signaling discomfort or defensiveness. Adjusting your approach accordingly can foster a more positive and productive conversation.

To enhance your nonverbal communication skills, practice in various settings and observe how others respond to your gestures. Pay attention to the messages your own body language sends and adapt as necessary. By harnessing the power of nonverbal communication, you can amplify the impact of your words and connect more effectively with others.

Active listening is an essential skill in effective communication that is often overlooked. It goes beyond simply hearing the words being said and involves fully engaging with the speaker and demonstrating genuine attentiveness. By unlocking the key to active listening, you can significantly enhance your communication skills and create more meaningful and productive conversations.

Active listening involves giving your undivided attention to the speaker, maintaining eye contact, and using verbal and nonverbal cues to show that you are fully engaged in the conversation. It also requires controlling your own internal dialogue and avoiding interrupting or finishing the speaker's sentences. Instead, focus on understanding their perspective and feelings.

By actively listening, you create an atmosphere of respect and trust, enabling both parties to openly express their thoughts and feelings. This encourages more in-depth and authentic conversations, fostering stronger connections and increasing understanding.

Active listening also helps to prevent misunderstandings and conflicts by ensuring that you have a clear understanding of the speaker's message.

Practicing active listening can be transformative in both personal and professional relationships. It allows you to connect on a deeper level, build rapport, and develop more meaningful connections. By unlocking this key aspect of effective communication, you open up a world of possibilities for building stronger relationships and achieving greater success in both your personal and professional life.

Thus a strong word is key to strong communication and a wide range of words opens up a multitude of possibilities for expressing yourself effectively, making your message more impactful and engaging. Moreover, using a word with proper (pressure) tone and time shows that you are well-educated and can command the attention of your audience or readers.

www.ingramcontent.com/pod-product-compliance
Ingram Content Group UK Ltd.
Pitfield, Milton Keynes, MK11 3LW, UK
UKHW061436190726
13845UKWH00023B/182
* 9 7 8 9 3 3 4 2 7 2 2 9 1 *